TIPS FOR COLLEGE FRESHMEN

124 Tips for Fun, Faith & Good Grades

Arliss Dickerson

INTRODUCTION

This Book comes out of talking to and watching hundreds of college freshmen. Some had a great four, five, or six years and some had a brief one or two semester stay. College can be the best time of your life and the worst time of your life....All in the same day!. It is a great and wonderful adventure. Like most adventures, the way it turns out is usually the result of the preparation and decisions that you make. College really can offer the best of having fun, growing in your faith, and reaching your full potential. Never forget there are people there to help you. But, you have to make a connection to them. Campus Christian groups, churches, and caring professors want to help you make it. College Ministers on campus and in local churches have given their lives to caring about and helping people just like you. Give them the chance to do so.

Jeremiah 29:11 says, "For I know the plans I have for you, declares the Lord, plans to prosper you and not to harm you, plans to give hope and a future." That is what college is all about. How it turns out is up to you. Hopefully, these brief tips will help you as your start your college adventure.

The tips are divided into three sections which are the tips from me, the second section is made up of brief tips from people just like you who were once freshmen and survived. The third section is tips from scripture that are great for encouragement and even to memorize. You can start at Tip #1 and read straight through or thumb through and pick the tips that are of the most interest or need to you at the moment. They are not in any numerical order. Some are "life changers" and others are just for making your day a little better.

This book is dedicated to my two favorite students, Victoria and Celia Mayfield.

Arliss Dickerson

arlissdickerson@gmail.com

CRAZY FACTS ABOUT COLLEGE

Students who live in dorms tend to make better grades than those who live in apartments.

More girls go to college than guys.

Students often borrow more money than they need and are stuck with large monthly payments almost immediately after graduation.

Students who live in smaller dorms tend to know more people and be happier than those who live in high rise dorms.

About 80% of college students change their major at least once.

More math majors change their major than any other.

You will marry someone you date.

Seven out of ten high school seniors active in church make no college spiritual connection.

College cafeterias have learned that the name of the dish affects students approval of it.

Most colleges now have first class workout facilities for students to use.

A large number of college cafeterias are open all times of the day and night.

Many students who live on campus still take on-line classes.

Parents cannot see their son or daughters' grades without the student's permission.

A RECIPE FOR COLLEGE SUCCESS

When your mom makes a dish you really like, it comes from a recipe. It tells what ingredients to mix together to have something good to eat. Here is the recipe for success at college.

There are three necessary ingredients:

1. **Intentional Priorities** – Decide what is important to you. Make those things the center of your activities at the start of school. If your faith matters to you, then that is a priority. Priorities help someone decide what to do and not do when there are lots of choice.
2. **Friends** – Everybody wants and needs friends. Your friends have a big influence in where you go and what you do. Make friends by your priorities. If your friends have similar priorities, you are more likely to continue to practice and live by those priorities. Some wise person has said, "We become like those we hang out with the most.
3. **Schedule** – One thing that goes a long way in determining the success of your college career is having a workable schedule that involves sleep, eating well, and studying. Be intentional in planning and living by a weekly schedule that has time for sleep, study, and fun. The more you function on a regular schedule, the more likely you are to be able to function at your best.

TEN YEARS FROM NOW?

Where do you want to be ten years from now? That may sound like a silly question just as you are starting college. But, here is the reality, decisions you will make freshman year will help determine where you can and cannot be in ten years. If you are convicted of a felony, that will remain on your record. Potential employers do background checks. A college town newspaper carried a story of a college freshman who was driving drunk at 4:00 a.m. and hit another vehicle. The driver of the other vehicle was killed. The freshman was jailed and charged with a serious crime. He likely will not be where he planned to be in ten years. Realize the importance of your decisions now. Your little decisions will pretty well determine your big decisions. Where do YOU want to be in ten years?

TIP #3

THE 5 DUMBEST MISTAKES FRESHMEN MAKE

A survey was done of one hundred students and they were asked, "What was the dumbest mistake you made as a freshman?"

Here are the 5 most frequent responses in reverse order:

5. **Making bad decisions** because of hanging out with the wrong people.

4. **Goofing off** at the beginning of the fall semester and getting too far behind.

3. **Not** taking college seriously.

2. **Not going** to class.

1. **Not getting involved** in campus activities and just hanging out with high school friends or staying in my room.

TIP #4

THE EASIEST WAY TO PASS A CLASS

The simplest and easiest thing to do to increase the likelihood of passing a class and even to make a good grade is to GO TO CLASS ALL THE TIME. Three things happen when you go to class. Many professors will lay out the whole course in front of you or at the very least, cover the basics. You will hear what you need to know. Second, you will not miss any pop tests and having those zeroes pile up in your grade average. Third, your being there demonstrates that you care and that matters to some professors. Studies show that students who attend class regularly make better grades and that the more often they attend increases the likelihood of a higher grade. And, the more frequently they miss class, the more likely they are to fail. Going to class is one of the secret tricks to college success.

TIP #5

HOW CAN I MAKE FRIENDS?

A high school senior said, "How can I make friends, if I go to a school where I don't already know anybody?" The first thing is to realize that you need friends and that you will need to do some intentional things to meet and make friends. The important thing is to make friends with people who will help you do and become what your goals are. Making the wrong friends can be destructive to your plans and college career. Make friends by your priorities, not priorities by your friends. The first week of school go to Welcome Week events on campus. Look for events that sound interesting to you. Students there are likely to share your interests. Introduce yourself to people. Don't leave it up to others. Introduce yourself to the people who live around you. Introduce yourself to people in your classes that sit close to you. When someone seems friendly and responds, ask them to go get coffee or a soda and talk about class or whatever. If being a Christian at college is important to you, always, ALWAYS check out and go to Christian events on campus or at nearby churches. AND, look for upper classmen who would be possible friends. They can help you navigate the first weeks because they already know things about the campus. Remember, that an older adult who is a campus or church College Minister can be a great friend of another generation. Plus, they can and will introduce you to other new friends. To have friends, be a friend!

TIP #6

PICKING YOUR FRIENDS

A college education is 50% books and 50% the things that you learn about doing life and relationships. Everyone goes to college looking for friends. Some make friends with the first people they meet or that live around them in dorms or apartments. A key to remember is that we tend to become like those with whom we hang out the most. Jim Rohm, the motivational speaker, has said that we become like the five people with whom we spend the most time. So, choose your friends by what is important to you. Is your faith important? Are good grades important to you? What about learning discipline and growing in maturity and decision making? Choose friends that exhibit characteristics that are among those attributes that you admire. Students who have Christian friends are more likely to grow in Christ likeness and Christian lifestyle. Those who have friends who study and make good grades are more likely to study and make good grades. You get the idea. Choose wisely!

TIP #7

FRIENDSHIPS SOMETIMES BREAK UP.

One of the great things about college is making new friends. But, sometimes those friendships or dating relationships break up for a variety of reasons. The important thing is to not let that throw you and disrupt your freshman year.

Remember this:

-Some friendships are just short term and that is okay.

-It is okay to not be best friends, but still have a positive relationship.

-Don't let the breakup of a friendship keep you from going to places and events that you want and need to attend to avoid possibly seeing them.

-Don't badmouth them to other friends.

-Think about whether there is anything you might learn from this breakup about how to do good relationships.

TIP #8

FORGIVENESS HELPS A LOT

f you are like most freshmen, you will make some mistakes either on personal issues or in class. Forgive yourself. Don't let guilt feelings keep you from going forward in a positive way. Friends and others will let you down sometimes. Forgive them and give them a second chance, until they have proven that they are not worthy of your trust and friendship. Hanging onto and nurturing anger toward another person only harms you. St. Augustine said, "Bitterness toward someone else is like drinking poison and hoping they die."

TIP #9

YOU GOTTA FIND YOUR GROUP OR GROUPS!

Several years back an informal study was done at one of the Ivy League colleges as to who the happiest students were. It turned out to be the members of the football team. That was surprising since Ivy League schools are known for academics, not their sports. As they dug into it, they found it had nothing to do with football. It was all about being part of a group that shared the same goals and priorities. Part of being happy in college is being part of a group that shares your goals and priorities. It can be the Chess Club or the band. And, you can be part of more than one group. Be intentional during the first days of school starting of finding and connecting with at least one group that is on the same page that you are. For a Christian, it is essential to be part of a Christian group. But, avoid the two extremes: some are part of no group and others try to be part of too many groups. Being part of a healthy group increases the likelihood of a great freshman year. Being part of a Christian group increases the likelihood of Christian growth and encouragement.

TIP #10

SHOULD I JOIN A SORORITY OR FRATERNITY?

Greek life is a big thing on some campuses and not so much on others. For some, it is a good experience and for others it is not. And, there are lots of students who have great college experiences without being a part of Greek life.

PROS:	CONS:
Helps you meet a lot of people.	Expense of monthly dues/fees
Lots of social or formal events	Time issues due to required events
Charitable projects done by each	

Things to Consider:

How like minded is the group to you in their activities and standards?

How do they relate to others who are not members?

Are they involved in anything other than Greek life?

Some Suggestions:

Ask a trusted upperclassman who has joined why they did and what they see as the benefits.

Ask a trusted upperclassman who did not join why they did not and why that has been best for them.

Consider not joining your first semester to allow time to adjust to school and to get an accurate view of each group and how you might fit.

TIP #11

WHY DATE AND HOW?

Dating is a way to get to know someone and as we do, we learn what we value in relationships. Plus, we learn what it takes to make guy/girl relationships work. It also helps us to see what we may or may not value in a future mate. Dates do not have to be a big deal. They don't have to cost a lot of money. It can be as simple as going for a hike or drinking a soda together. But, here is an important thing to remember: **We marry someone that we date.** If you realize that someone you are dating is someone that you would never marry, it is wise to stop that dating relationship. Someone can be a good person and even fun, but they are not someone to enter into a lifelong relationship. The longer a couple dates the more it becomes a habit and there will be pressures from friends and family to go ahead and take the next step of marriage. Maybe, you did not date much or any in high school, but now as you are making new friends is the time to widen your relationships. Ask that nice guy or girl, if they would like to go for a run or to drink a cup of coffee and visit. The worst that can happen is they can say no. But, they can say yes too.

TIP #12

7 RED FLAGS IN A DATING RELATIONSHIP

Apart from just being fun, dating in college is one way you learn about yourself, about others, and what is important to you in a relationship. Dating is not just to find someone to marry. But, there are some very clear RED FLAGS to know. A Red Flag is a warning.....it means BEWARE, there is danger close. It may mean get out of that relationship or it may mean in order for it to be a healthy relationship some changes need to be made.

Here are the Red Flags and any one can be a sign to run the other direction:

1. **The two of you are all consumed in each other and other relationships are neglected.** The problem with this type relationship is that no one person can or should meet all of another person's emotional and relational needs. It limits personal growth.
2. **Major differences are ignored or not talked about such as future goals, religious differences and life priorities.** Part of what makes relationships work and grow is being on the same page about goals and priorities. If those cannot be talked about, it is not a mature and lasting relationship.
3. **There is a drastic change in the sense of responsibility one or both partners have to other commitments.** This often leads to burnout due to lack of balance in life and to trouble in other areas such as grades, jobs, etc. A healthy relationship makes you a better you.
4. **Friends or family strongly disapprove of your partner.** When those who know you best and love you most do not approve of the relationship, it may mean they are seeing something you are not seeing or choosing to ignore.
5. **Conflict is avoided at all cost or not resolved in a healthy way.** If disagreements must be avoided or one partner has to always "win" to maintain the relationship, it is probably one not worth keeping.
6. **One partner uses, abuses, or demonstrates a lack of respect for the other.** Any time one partner hits the other or does physical harm in any way, that is a deal breaker. Sometimes, it is not physical, but emotional in that one has to dominate the other or regularly put them down. Walk away!

7. **Physical contact or sexual involvement becomes the central activity or the main part of the relationship.** Physical or sexual involvement cannot maintain a relationship. Also, the more the relationship becomes physical, the harder it is to know what your true feelings are. Do you love this person or simply love what you are doing?

TIP #13

DON'T DATE SOMEONE YOU WOULD NOT MARRY!!

National studies show that pretty well everyone marries someone they date. Dumb right? Nobody goes on a first date planning to marry that person. But, the longer we date someone the more likely we are to marry that person. A girl or guy can be fun to date and nice looking, but they do not share the same life priorities or goals that you do. Sometimes, first, or second or, fifteenth dates need to be last date. One of the purposes of dating is to get to know others. When we know someone is on a different page than we are, that is a good thing to learn. That experience and time dating has not been wasted. It has probably helped us understand ourselves better and what is important to us. But, it is time to move on. Do not keep dating someone out of habit or just to have a date. Admit when it is time to call it quits. You cannot get to a good relationship until you get out of one that is leading nowhere good.

TIP #14

WHY SHOULD I NOT DATE A NON-CHRISTIAN???

Part of the fun of college is all the great new people that you meet. And, it is easy to meet someone that can be fun to date. After one or two dates or just getting to know the other person, you may learn that they are not a Christian, So, what is wrong with dating them, you might say. The longer you date someone the easier it is to get attached to them and even to come to love them. That may lead to thoughts or talk of marriage. Being a Christian should affect all our decisions and priorities. The more we give of our life to someone who does not share that basic commitment, the easier it becomes to turn away from our faith and Christian lifestyle. **But, if I date them, that may help them become a Christian, one might say.** One college guy said, "I used to not date Christian girls because I knew they would not want to do what I wanted to. But, I learned, if I would go to church with them, then they would be more willing to do the things I wanted to do." It is easy to begin to make compromises in our commitments, when we care about someone. We want to please them. Christians should be friends with non-Christians, but regularly dating someone who does not share your beliefs can lead to tough choices or compromises that are harmful.

TIP #15

REASONS TO BREAK OFF A DATING RELATIONSHIP

It is possible for a couple to be in a dating relationship, but is really an unhealthy one and could be harmful either now or later. So, what are some deal breakers for a relationship?

1. **Lack of trust -** If you realize that your dating partner is being dishonest with you, it is time to walk away. No matter how fun or attractive the person is, their dishonesty will hurt you at some point.
2. **Abuse –** When a person is abusive in their actions toward you either physically or verbally, it is a relationship that should not be continued. It is easy to tell yourself that it will get better. It usually does not and often gets worse the longer the relationship goes on.
3. **Different standards –** If your partner has a different set of moral standards than you do and is pushing you to do things you believe are wrong, it is time to get out. There will continually be conflict or you will eventually give into demands and violate your own moral code. At the very least, you will lower your standards.

TIP #16

GROWING YOUR RELATIONSHIPS DEEPER

All of us have many acquaintances and some friends. Friends are those people that we enjoy being around and could even call on when we need help. Jerzy Gregorek, author of "The Happy Body", has said, "Negative people are like drains and positive people are like fountains." Many people develop lifelong friendships in college. So, how do we grow these kind of lasting friendships?

Colossians 3:12-13 lists 6 Relationship Builders:

1. **Compassion –** This is to care about the other person's feelings and to be willing to hurt with them when they hurt and celebrate with them when they have a victory.
2. **Kindness –** To be kind to someone is simply to do little things for them that encourage them or make their life better.
3. **Humility –** When we are humble, it means not always putting our own wants and preferences first in the relationship.
4. **Gentleness –** Our language, as well as our behavior and actions, can be rough or hurtful. A gentle friend is one who is not hurtful in word or deed….even when teasing.
5. **Patience –** Sometimes, we just put up with each other a little bit. Patience in a relationship means that everything does not have to happen on our terms or timing.

6. **Forgiveness** – Even the best mess up and we must be able to forgive them and let it go. When we forgive, we do not keep score. To receive forgiveness, we must be willing to extend it.

"Therefore as God's chosen people, holy and dearly loved, clothe yourselves with compassion, kindness, humility, gentleness, and patience. Bear with each other and forgive whatever grievances you may have against one another. Forgive as the Lord forgave you." Colossians 3:12-13

TIP #17

HELP, MY FRIEND IS NOT A CHRISTIAN

You will probably meet and connect with a wide variety of students. Some of them may not be a Christian and have maybe never even heard or know that God loves them. So, what can you tell them? Here are some simple steps.

1. **Tell them your story.** Explain that you have not always been a Christian, but that you made an intentional decision to ask Christ into your life.
2. **Nothing can cause God not to love them.** Some think they have done things so bad that God could not care for or forgive them.
3. **Share some scripture such as:**
   Romans 3:23 "All have sinned and fall short of the glory of God."
   Romans 6:23 "The gift of God is eternal life."
   Romans 10:9 "If you confess with your mouth and believe in your heart."
   Romans 10:13 "Everyone who calls on the name of the Lord will be saved."
4. **Ask if they would like to pray in their own words and ask Christ into their life.**
5. **If they pray, connect them to someone like your College Minister.**

Some will respond to your sharing this good news and some will not. That is not up to you. When you share to the best of your ability, you have done great. Continue to be their friend and encourage them regardless of how they respond. God may work over a period of time.

TIP #18

LIVING AT HOME

Many studies have shown that students who live on campus tend to make better grades than students who live away. So, what is the deal? Is there something magic on those dorm walls? Here is the deal, it is easier for students who live on campus to feel and act like a college student. Plus, it is no big deal for them to go to the Library or to a study group. Proximity is part of it. The second part is, campus is where their relationships are. If you are planning to

ive at home, you are not doomed to make poor grades or hate college. You just need to decide
o be a student at that college and not just someone who happens to go there for classes.

Things You Can Do:

1. **Participate** in some club or activity.
2. **Develop some friends** on campus and do not just hang out with friends from home
   or your former high school.
3. **Schedule** some time each week that you will study in the library. That gives quick
   access to reference material, but also develops a regular study pattern.
4. **Buy a meal ticket** or deposit some money in a campus account to eat some of your
   meals on campus where other students eat. Friends are made over food!

Make the intentional choice to be a student of that college....not just someone taking classes
here.

TIP #19

SAFETY ON CAMPUS

College campuses work at keeping students safe. Yet, each student must be aware and be
responsible for their own safety. Many campuses now issue a campus wide alert by text
message, if an incident happens on campus. Take these alerts seriously and avoid placing
yourself in dangerous or risky situations.

Practice these safety habits:

1. **Record the Campus Police number** in your phone.
2. **Be aware** of escort and ride services that many campuses offer at night.
3. **Walk in a group** late at night, when possible.
4. **Report dorm safety issues** such as someone propping outside doors open for others
   to enter.
5. **Emergency Button Stations** are located on many campuses. Know where they are.
6. **A tear gas spray** can be attached to a key ring.
7. **Comply with a robber's requests** and do not force a greater confrontation.

TIP #20

CHOOSING A DORM OR APARTMENT

Often freshmen have no choice where they will live, if they are not commuting from home.
Residence Life assigns students to a location and that settles it. Other times, there are some
choices. Or, living in an apartment off campus may be an option. So, what do you choose?

Factors to Consider:

1. **The best reason** to live in a campus dorm or residence is ease in meeting lots of other students.
2. **Students tend** to be happier overall in smaller dorms as opposed to high rise dorms. The larger a dorm is, the easier it is to feel like a number and lost in the crowd.
3. **The farther** an apartment is from campus, the more tempting it is to not take the time and effort to go back for a study group, fun event, whatever.
4. **Campus housing** often provides things that cost extra in apartments such as cable, wifi, etc.
5. **An apartment** can offer more privacy and less interruptions.
6. An apartment can be **good preparation** for living on your own after college.
7. **Dorms** often provide special events, intramural teams, etc for their residents.
8. **A major consideration** is to ask, "Which option is the safest?"

TIP #21

RAPE ON COLLEGE CAMPUSES

Unfortunately, college women are twice as likely to be sexually assaulted as robbed and 13% of all students experience rape or sexual assault in some way (statistics from Rape, Abuse & Incest National Network). This does not mean you should function in fear on campus, but it does mean that you need to be aware of the reality and act accordingly. Most college sexual assaults involve one or more being drunk and usually happens with someone they know.

1. **Do not go alone** to someone's room or apartment you have just met.
2. **Do not leave a drink unattended** at a party or public gathering and then drink from it.
3. **Understand** that when you are drinking alcohol that you are more vulnerable.
4. **Immediately** get out of situations that begin to feel threatening.
5. **Be strong and forceful** in your first response to any unwanted physical advances.
6. **Report any sexual assault** to authorities and seek medical attention. Your report can help prevent this from happening to someone else.

TIP #22

GETTING ALONG WITH A ROOMMATE

Some are able to pick their roommate and others simply get whomever the school assigns. Even in rooming with someone you have known previously, there can be surprises that come.

Suggestions for Roommate Happiness:

1. **At the beginning,** talk about individual preferences about studying in the room, who goes to bed when, etc.
2. **A frequent point of unhappiness** between roommates is when to have guests in the room, how long they stay, etc. It is essential to have this discussion at the start.
3. **What about borrowing** clothes and other personal items?
4. **When do overhead lights** need to be out or when can they come on in the morning?
5. **If there is food in the room or apartment,** what is for either's use and what is private?
6. **Who** cleans what and when?

TIP #23

ROOMMATE UNHAPPINESS

If there are continuing roommate issues or unhappiness, check with the Residence Life office, to see what the options are. Some schools have an official No Questions Asked Roommate Change Week. If this seems to be a possible need, check on it early in order to not miss the deadline. But, when changing do some advance work to make sure the change will be beneficial. All roommate changes are not necessarily better. Remember, that if there are things your roommate does that irritates or makes things inconvenient for you, there may be thing you are doing that affect your roommate in a negative way. Being sensitive to and improving your own behavior may improve the behavior of your roommate.

TIP #24

MAKE YOUR BED AND DO YOUR LAUNDRY!

A great book to read (and it is short) is "Make Your Bed" by former Navy Seal, Admiral William McRaven. It is full of super practical advice. Two things: First, by making your bed, you have started the day with an accomplishment. Second, if your dorm or apartment is your new home, you want it to be inviting and comfortable. Nobody does well living in a mess. Determine that your room will be reasonably neat and comfortable for you. The setup and appearance of your room is a reflection you and your personality. Who do you want to be at college? Make your room/apartment representative of who you want to be and it will encourage that happening. Besides, getting into a made bed at night is way more inviting than climbing into a mess. Oh yeah, wash your sheets every week! That usually happens best when you have a set day and time that is laundry day and time. Waiting till you "feel like it" does not work well. Very few freshmen get overwhelmed with the great desire to do laundry.

TIP #25

DIRTY LAUNDRY HAPPENS

If you have worn your clothes as many different ways as possible and yes, some freshmen have turned their underwear wrong side out, it is time to admit that laundry has to be done. If you have never done laundry before, try these hints, before you call home and admit you are clueless.

Some Laundry Guidelines:

1. **Read** the labels to make sure no garments have special care instructions.
2. **Make sure** all the pockets are empty. Tissues make a big mess!
3. **It is better** to wash darks and whites separately.
4. **When in doubt** what temperature to use, use **COLD WATER.**
5. **Follow detergent instructions** on how much to use. Too much is bad.
6. **Don't** wash towels and clothes together. Lint gets on the clothes.
7. **Be careful** to not over dry as some garments can shrink.

TIP #26

BUYING BOOKS

Books are one of the crazy expenses at the start of school. First, check on used books that students are selling from the previous year. Often, there are notices posted on bulletin boards, Just make sure they are the current edition that the professor will be using. There are a variety of sources of new books. There may be multiple book stores and it is wise to compare prices at the different stores. Do not assume they are the same. Some students have had success going on line to the publisher and buying the books for significantly less than they were offered at the local stores. Occasionally, an enterprising student will be able to find some textbooks at the campus library that can be checked out. But, that is very rare. The point is to save money by checking multiple sources.

TIP #27

LOOK FOR STUDENT DISCOUNTS

Many businesses (especially fast food restaurants) in college towns offer college student discounts. Check out the campus paper for those that advertise student discounts. Many will hand out flyers on campus with coupons during the first few days of the fall semester. When buying something in a store, ask if they offer a student discount. If so, they will sometimes ask to see your ID card. College student budgets go farther when you look for and use student discounts.

TIP #28

FRESHMEN ORIENTATION/REGISTRATION

Many colleges have Summer Orientations and often have Pre-registration at these events. **Go to the first one you are eligible to attend.** If students are allowed to register at these events, the earlier you go, the greater choice you have in what classes to take and **When** to take them. There will be lots of 7:00 a.m. and unwanted night classes still open later in the summer or when school starts. Prime time classes will be full. Also, going to Summer Orientation helps you connect with other students who could be a friend and you have the summer to talk, etc. It is even possible to connect with a potential roommate. Those who do not care or are not serious about college tend to go as late as possible. Find out if there is an optional pre-school leadership retreat or workshop that you can attend. This gives you a head start on making friends and it sets you up for opportunities with those faculty and staff who run student activities and organizations.

TIP #29

REALITY WEEK

Reality Week is a term you may not hear, but you will probably experience it. Reality Week happens middle way of the second week or into the third week of the semester. It is the time that all those fun Welcome Week parties and free pizza events have gone away. And, there comes that first test for which you are not prepared and you fail it or do not make the grade you are accustomed to making. Reality Week brings the realization that this is not summer camp. It is serious college. Many freshmen have one of two extreme reactions. One is to drop everything and go to class and back to your room. Or, it is too late I have already ruined my college career, so it does not matter what I do now. Both are wrong! Rather, this is the time to sit down and figure out a reality schedule that allows time for class, study, sleep, and some fun, encouraging activities. Studies show that students active in campus activities are more likely to be happy, stay in school, and graduate. So, Reality Week is not the time to throw in the towel on life or college, but it is time to get on a balanced schedule. You can do it!

TIP #30

RUN FOR A FRESHMAN OFFICE

One way to connect with others and find a place on campus is to run for a freshman office. It is fairly normal for Student Governments have Freshmen Senators or Representative positions and they are elected during those first few weeks. Other campuses elect Freshmen Class officers. Run for office. It is alright to lose. That point is that it will help you meet others and it will help those who run student activities to be aware of who you are. Running for office gives you an excuse to talk to other students and ask them to vote for you. Go to the Student Activities Office the first week and find out what positions might be available. Many Christian ministries have Freshmen Leadership Teams. Go to the College Minister on campus or at a college friendly church and ask, if they have a Freshmen Leadership Team. These teams or groups are often selected from those who have shown interest. Being part of such a group will connect you to other freshmen who have a desire to grow in their faith.

TIP #31

FRESHMAN FLU

About the fourth or fifth week of the fall semester you may get a funny feeling in the pit of your stomach that says, "I would rather be at home than in college." Wait, is that homesickness? No, only kids who go to camp for the first time get homesick. Right? What you probably have is the Freshman Flu. The Freshman Flu comes as a result of being somewhere brand new where you do not know everybody like you did in high school. The new is wearing off and the professors don't know your name and don't seem to care that they don't know it. It is normal to get that feeling. Here is the thing: **Don't let it control you or make your decisions.** This form of flu says to sit in your room and be miserable and that just causes it to get worse. Don't pack your bag or check out of the dorm and head home. Call a new friend you met the last week or two and tell them it is time to eat tacos or split a pizza. Do something with someone. If you have not met anyone you feel comfortable calling, go the to the campus Christian Center or a college ministry church (even if you have not been before) and find out about an intramural team you might could play on or one of their small groups that you could join. Find out what they offer just for a freshman like you. Nobody talks about Freshman Flu, but it is real and if you get moving, it will not beat you. You will beat it!

TIP #32

GIVE IT A SEMESTER

Statistics tell us that one third of college freshmen do not come back for their sophomore year. Almost every freshman wants to quit sometime during that first semester. Psychologists say that the two greatest times of change in a person's life are birth to age one and high school graduation till Christmas. No wonder you feel some stress and strain. It is a normal feeling during a time of great adjustment. Determine that you will finish that first semester no matter what. If you think you are at the wrong school, don't make the final decision to transfer until the semester is over. Make no decisions about quitting, moving home or transferring until you have completed the fall semester. Talk with an older adult other than your parents that you trust about your feelings. Sometimes, talking to parents too early in the process causes them unnecessary anxiety about what you will do. School counselors, College Ministers, and staff at your church would love to listen and talk with you about it. Getting your feelings and concerns out often helps you see them more realistically. Consider if you need to adjust your schedule, to get more fun activities, relaxation, sleep, study time or whatever into your routine. Whatever you do, do not quit going to class and or just isolate in your room. Get out and make a new friend. Lots of freshmen who have wanted to quit at some point in the semester have wound up not wanting to go home at Christmas. Don't quit just because you feel like quitting.

TIP #33

PICKING A MAJOR

How do you know if a major fits you and will be a degree that you will complete? Many freshmen say they picked a major because they were told there were lots of job in that field. Or, they were told that people in that profession make lots of money. While both things can be true, it is not an indicator of the right major for you. When considering a major, one way to evaluate it in regards to its fit for you is to look at the required classes listed in that major. Do those classes sound of interest to you? It is not whether they sound hard or not. But, do they sound like something you would like to know more about? Do they fit the way you think and how you see yourself working some day? For example, if you hate math, majoring in something that requires a lot of math may not make sense for you. If Chemistry in high school was almost the death of you, a major with lots of Chemistry may not be for you. Sometimes a good clue to what major will work best comes from taking a variety of introductory courses and see what clicks for you. Beware of someone else picking your major for you. You are the one that will live and work with that decision. Remember every time you change your major, you usually increase your time in school and the expenses that go with it. Beware of money or prestige being your guiding principle for choosing a major.

TIP #34

LISTEN TO YOUR ADVISOR...HOWEVER

Each college student has an Academic Advisor. It may be one because a student has designated a certain major or it may be a general advisor assigned at random. An Academic Advisor's purpose is to help a student know what they must take to meet school requirements and to be able to graduate with the desired degree. They usually suggest classes to take and when to take them. When is very important. Some courses must be taken in a certain order and not all classes are offered every semester. If a student gets out of order on classes, it can cause a one or two semester delay while waiting on a particular class to be offered. Yes, students have spent an extra semester or even an extra year in college due to not taking the right classes at the time they were offered. So, listen to your Academic Advisor....**HOWEVER**.....if an Advisor makes a mistake or tells a student something that is not to their benefit, it is not the Advisor that suffers the consequences. Do not just blindly do what the Advisor suggests. Advocate for you, ask questions, and double check all academic decisions. Most Advisors care and genuinely are trying to help, but even the best make mistakes. You are the one responsible for you. Double check those decisions and it is always possible to request a new Advisor, if it becomes necessary.

TIP #35

FIND THE LIBRARY

Colleges spend a lot of money on their library. They feel like it is beneficial to a college education. With the internet and google, some students never go to the library. That is a mistake. Check out the library during the first week of classes. Besides all sorts of reference materials, it is a good place to go and study. Often, it is in the center of campus and is easy to get to between classes where you can go between classes and read the material that was just assigned. Many campus libraries have rooms that can be used and even reserved for study groups to meet. In a few instances, students have even found copies of a required text there and did not have to buy it. It is not unusual for a library to offer copy services at a reasonable price or even to allow some copies for free. See what your campus library has to offer. You may be surprised and helped.

TIP #36

WEBSITES CAN BE HELPFUL

Websites can be another great resource to tap into that are fair and legitimate helps for college students. Students often hear about and are tempted to use those sites that are selling term papers, etc. That is cheating and is often caught by professors and leads to a failing grade. But, don't let that keep you from using the honest resources available. Before using any services of a website, make sure to know, if it is free or what the cost will be. Ask friends about what ones they have found and use.

Check out these and look for others:

YOUR Campus Library Website – Helpful information about the library and other helps are posted there.

Google Calendar – It will help you organize for tests, due dates, etc.

Word Hippo – A Thesaurus can help you see related words or ones that can be substituted for each other.

Rocket Resume – An attractive and well done resume goes a long way toward helping get that part time job, scholarship, internship, etc.

Nerdify – Find the answer to some question.

TIP #37

DON'T LOSE YOUR BALANCE

"Don't lose your balance." Is advice usually given to someone walking on a beam or high up on a cliff. But, many college freshmen mess up their freshmen year by losing their balance. The Bible says in Luke 2:52 describing Jesus, **"Jesus grew in wisdom and stature, and in favor with God and men."** That is describing the perfect balance in all parts of Jesus' life. He grew physically, intellectually, in His human relationships and in His relationship to the Lord. Part of making college work is not losing sight of any of these four areas. In your life, it refers to your relationship to the Lord, your friendships, your class work, and your physical which is the wise care of your body. Ignoring one or more of these will get you in trouble. Yet, no one of these is to be your total point of emphasis. Usually, one or two of these will come naturally to you and one or two take some extra work and attention. Jesus lived a perfect life and you will not. But, working at some balance in these four areas will go a long way toward a really good freshman year. Be honest with yourself where you might need some help and encouragement. And, don't let the one you are best at overwhelm the others.

TIP #38

WHAT ABOUT ADVANCED CLASSES FIRST SEMESTER?

Because of taking college classes while in high school or testing out of some basics, it is possible to take advanced classes during the first semester of college. Here is why sometimes that is not a good idea. The first semester of freshman year is a time of big adjustments. Starting in upper class courses can increase the pressure. Also, taking these tougher classes at the beginning can cause a hit on your grade point that affects scholarship retention and even grad school admission later on. Another issue is the possibility of changing your major later and those classes not being beneficial in the new major. If at all possible, it is usually wise to take required basics during that first semester. Besides, lot of students have hated taking freshmen courses their senior year that they skipped over at the beginning of college.

TIP #39

DROPPING OR ADDING A CLASS

If you are a fulltime student, it is important to realize that there are different things tied to that classification. A student must be taking a certain number of hours to be classified as fulltime. To drop below that number of hours or classes can affect your status in different situations. At some schools, it is required to be a fulltime student in order to live in school housing. Some require a student to be fulltime in order to receive and continue to receive a scholarship. Car Insurance cost is sometimes tied to a college student being classified as fulltime. Students have had insurance canceled as a result of dropping a class. Others have had to move out of campus housing or lost their scholarship. Colleges have a period early in the semester when classes can be dropped or added. Make sure that you know what that deadline is. There are lots of valid reasons for dropping a class. It may not be what the title seemed to say, etc. So, it is possible during these early days to drop one and add another that is more beneficial. Do not drop a class to add one until you are certain you can get into the class you are wanting to add. It is possible to drop one and not be able to get into another which leaves you in no man's land and short of hours. If possible, add the class first and then drop the unwanted class. Another reason some students drop a class is they realize very early they will not make a satisfactory grade. Dropping before the drop deadline usually means the class will not show up on the official transcript. Dropping later in the semester may cause it to show up on the transcript as "Dropped Passing" or "Dropped Failing". Never just stop attending a class and plan to drop it at some point. Drop it as soon as that decision is made. Too many students have forgotten to go through the official drop process and then to see that class and a failing grade show up on their record at the end of the semester. Policies and procedures vary from campus to campus. Be sure you know the Drop/Add policy and dates at your school.

TIP #40

PORN IS A TRAP!

A trap that many college students fall into is looking at pornography. Or, it may be a trap that you have already fallen into. Experts tell us that pornography is more addictive than alcohol, marijuana, and drugs. What that means is that despite your intentions or plans, if you look at it, you are likely to become addicted. So, what is the big deal? A porn habit is destructive to healthy guy/girl relationships and later can be the cause of the death of a marriage. It can begin to consume all our time. Porn is not just a guy trap as more and more young women are becoming addicted. It is a trap that claims most who look at it. If you have not, do not go near it.

What if I am already in the trap? First, get with a school counselor, a trusted mentor such as your College Minister, or a Christian counselor and admit your situation. That is the first step. Second, make plans that will help you beat this destructive habit. There are different apps available that you can use that will allow someone else to see what you are looking at on your phone or computer or that will block it. Make sure you are aware of the cost of one time use or regular subscription cost of any of these apps.

Here are some to check out:

X3watch – It provides detailed reports and sends notifications to selected persons as to what you have watched which will help them hold you accountable.

BlockerX – This allows you to block a large number of pornographic websites and also blocks certain key words.

Accountable2You – Users can assign different accountability partners to each individual device. It sends weekly use reports as well as instant notification to your designated accountability partners.

TIP #41

WHAT ABOUT ALCOHOL?

The use of alcohol on college campuses is common practice. It is wise to make a decision in advance what your practice will be. Many who have never used alcohol before become involved during the first weeks of school simply trying to fit into social activities and be accepted by new friends. **Why is alcohol use a negative?** Depending on the state and local laws, many freshmen are not of legal drinking age. So, it is technically a crime. Some things we know about alcohol is it that it can be addictive and that most cases of rape on college campuses involve on or both parties being drunk. So, it can be dangerous. The Bible speaks against drunkenness. Since the Bible speaks against it, there must be a reason. Quite simply, anything that controls us apart from our relationship to the Lord is harmful. You might not be involved in a rape or become an alcoholic, but do you want to be controlled by the use of something that can be harmful to you or others? Also, your use of alcohol can be an encouragement to others. Even if you are able to control it, what about those who follow your example? Decide in advance what your practice will be and why.

TIP #42

WHAT ABOUT SEX?

With the freedom and privacy that college can bring and there being lots of guys and girls, sexual involvement is a possibility. Where do you fit in that? The Bible indicates that sexual involvement outside of marriage is wrong. But, WHY does it say that? Anytime the Bible speaks against something, it is because that behavior is harmful to one or all those involved. Sex is a creation of God and so, it is not evil or dirty. It was created by God to help bind two people together. If two people are not prepared to make a commitment to each other, do they need to become more bound together? Two negative possibilities from sexual involvement are an unwanted pregnancy and disease. A less obvious but powerful negative is sexual involvement makes it more difficult to decide if this person is someone you love and would possibly marry. Or, are you simply in love with the feelings of sexual involvement? If you have been sexually involved in high school, that does not have to determine what your practice will be from this day forward. Decide who you are today and move on from there. "Flee from sexual immorality. All other sins a man commits are outside his body, but he who sins sexually sins against his own body." I Corinthians 6:18

TIP #43

DEALING WITH TEMPTATION

Everyone is tempted. The Bible says that Jesus was tempted...really, it does. So, being tempted is not wrong in itself. The wrong comes when we give into a hurtful or harmful temptation. The first important thing in dealing with our temptations is to be honest with ourself about what is really a personal temptation. Then, you have to make a choice to not put yourself in situations that highlight that temptation. For example, if you have decided you will not drink alcohol, then it is not wise to go to an event where alcohol is the main entertainment. If you are tempted to sexual involvement with your boyfriend or girlfriend, then make decisions in advance about where you will and will not go on your dates or free time together. Perhaps, a long evening alone in one of your rooms is the not the best plan for a date. If cheating on a test is a temptation, then choosing where to sit or not sit may be a needed advance decision. Yielding to a temptation does not mean you are weak or terrible. Learn from that mistake and let it guide you in your future decisions and actions. You will be tempted by different harmful things the rest of your life, so now is a good time to start learning how to deal with it in advance.

"Then Jesus was led by the Spirit into the desert to be tempted by the devil." Matthew 4:1

TIP #44

I MESSED UP BAD….REAL BAD!!!

All of us mess up and sometimes we mess up really badly. It can easily happen at college when everything is new and there are new temptations. Plus, there is no one there to tell us not to do it. It may even be something that has been totally opposite to your moral code. So, what do you do when you have done something you should not have done?

1. **The first step** is to admit it to yourself that you messed up and need to make it right.
2. **Realize and determine** that does not define who you will be from this day forward. Don't give up on you. Make it a learning experience.
3. **I John 1:9** says, "If we confess our sins, he is faithful and just and will forgive us our sins and purify us from all unrighteousness."
4. **If you wronged** another person, acknowledge that to them and apologize.
5. **If necessary**, talk with a trusted counselor like a College Minister to help you sense forgiveness and to see the best path forward.
6. **Make any necessary** changes in habits, relationships, or places you go that might help this happen again.

TIP #45

ARE YOU A PRODIGAL SON OR DAUGHTER?

In Luke 15 is the story Jesus told commonly call, The Prodigal Son. It tells of a young man who left home and went away to live totally opposite of everything he had believed and been raised to practice. At the end of the story, he realizes his mistake and comes home to a loving father who welcomes him. Many high school students due to the craziness of senior year, school responsibilities, part time jobs, etc. have gone away from a strong connection to their faith and the church. Do you fit into that category? If you do, it does not have to be a permanent decision and define who you are in college. Simply admit the reality of where you are now faith and faith practice wise and make some specific commitments and decisions about how your faith will be central to you in college. Remember, what you do the first 2 or 3 weeks often determine your whole college career. If you want to read the whole story of The Prodigal, you can find it in Luke 15:11-32. By the way, it also tells of his brother who kept all the rules, but was not right in his heart. It is possible to have never missed a youth group meeting or summer camp, yet not be right in your heart. Resolve where you are now and where you want to be in your relationship to the Lord.

"But while he was still a long way off, his father saw him and was filled with compassion for him: he ran to his son, threw his arms around him and kissed him." Luke 15:20

TIP #46

DOUBTS ABOUT YOUR FAITH ARE NORMAL

Part of college is being exposed to different people and different ideas. This will include different ideas about faith. It is not unusual or weird for Christian students to have doubts about faith during freshman year. Some of the great believers in the Bible went through a time of doubt. Understanding the causes of doubt can help in facing and dealing with it.

Common causes:

1. **New information** or questions I cannot answer.
2. Nice and very **sincere people** who believe differently.
3. **A personal foul-up** or mistake that causes someone to question the validity of their faith.
4. **A bad happening** such as a loved one dying like a parent or grandparent. How could God let that happen?

There are three common ways students handle doubts. Some just throw up their hands and give up on faith. Others ignore their doubts and go through the motions of faith. The best choice is to be honest about it and face it. Almost always, your faith will come out stronger.

TIP #47

FOUR TIPS FOR FACING DOUBTS ABOUT FAITH

1. **Remember,** just because you do not know an answer to a tough question does not mean there is not an answer.

2. **Not everything** a professor or friend say about the Bible that raises questions and doubts is accurate.
3. **Keep hanging out** with other believers who will encourage and help. A common goof is to drop out of Christian activities until it is resolved. That is like checking out of a hospital until you get well.
4. **Ask people** who know more than you do. Talk to a wise mentor such as a College Minister who has spent their life studying and answering these kind of tough questions.

"I do believe; help me overcome my unbelief." Mark 9:24

TIP #48

REASONS TO BELIEVE

You may have become a Christian because your parents believed or because an adult such as your Youth Minister or a Sunday School teacher was a great friend to you. But, now that you are in college and growing in your knowledge, why should you believe as a Christian as a young adult?

1. The **complexity of our planet** with its check and balances points to a deliberate design.
2. **The Bible** was written over 1500 years by about 40 different people (30 Old Testament and 10 New Testament) but it shows a unity of message.
3. Even **non-Christian scholars** acknowledge the reality of Jesus as a person who existed in history.
4. The belief of Jesus' earliest followers in **his resurrection transformed them** into people willing to die for their faith.

TIP #49

MAKING GOOD DECISIONS

Part of growing up and becoming an adult is learning to make good decisions. Some wise person has said, "We make our decisions and then our decisions make us." In other words, we are a result of the **choices** and decisions that we make.

Seven Guidelines for making good decisions:

1. **Get accurate** information. Many poor decisions are made as a result of having incomplete information or inaccurate facts. Go to someone who is knowledgeable or works in that area to get accurate information.

2. **Consider if** this decision is consistent with your goals and plans for the future. Sometimes, a decision is as simple as, do I study or go out tonight. If the grade in this class can affect your future plans, is going out consistent with your future plan?
3. **Consider how** your decision affects others. Our family and friends care about us and can be affected by our choices. Does this decision affect those I care about?
4. **What** is the cost of this decision? Every choice and action has a cost. It can be in time, money, relationships, etc. Some choices are not wrong, they just are not worth what they cost.
5. **Learn** from your dumb decisions. We all make dumb decisions and choices. But, not everyone learns from those mistakes. Is there anything in the past that would shed some light on this decision?
6. **When possible,** on a big decision, lay out your thinking before a trusted friend and advisor before taking action on that decision. Expressing that decision and why out loud may help you see it in a better light. Plus, that person may be able to point out some things you have not considered.
7. **Is this decision** consistent with your beliefs and commitments as a Christian?

Tip #50

GO TO BREAKFAST

It is easy to get up late and run to that first class without eating breakfast, especially if you have been up late the night before cramming for a test. Dr. Gregory W. Phillips, at Blinn College in Texas, found that more students failed his Biology exams who had NOT eaten breakfast. Web MD says, "Many studies have linked eating breakfast to good health including better memory and brain power." Going to breakfast first simply helps you function better in the morning. If going to the cafeteria is not an option or super inconvenient, keep something in your room to eat that will not have your internal tank on empty in that first class or two of the day.

TIP #51

ASK ABOUT PROFESSORS

Who teaches a class can make all the difference in the world. When signing up for classes or considering switching a class, ask about the different professors who teach the classes. Who seems to care about their students? Who make the class interesting? Who best covers the material and prepares students for the related classes that come after it? Do not just ask, who is the easiest. Taking an easy class may feel good at the moment, but jam you up when you take an upperclass course that builds on the earlier one. When another student says they do not like a professor, ask why. Sometimes, that professor is not liked by some because they expect a lot and really teach the course well. An easy A is not always the best outcome. Ask about professors.

TIP #52

KEEP A CALENDAR

College professors are funny. The first class or two they will tell you some dates when things are due way up in the semester and expect you to remember them. Or, they will hand out something called a syllabus and it has information about the whole semester like when big tests will be and when a major paper is due. But, that first week or two you are trying to remember the name of that good looking guy or girl you met the other day. So, here is the thing, KEEP A CALENDAR! Obviously, you can plug dates into your phone or you can keep an old fashioned paper calendar stuck on your dorm room wall or in your room at home. Some do BOTH. Not only put down the dates when a test will be or when that paper is due, but put down a reminder some days ahead of that. Getting a reminder on your phone thirty minutes before a test you did not remember to study for is not too helpful. Usually, a term paper written the night before is not an A paper. **Read your Syllabus.** One professor put instructions for where he had hidden some money for anyone who found it on the second page of the Syllabus. By the end of the semester, no one had claimed the money. Lots of freshmen flunk their first test because they forgot or did not know when it was going to happen.

TIP #53

THE $10,000 SUGGESTION

A student was struggling in a class and knew that her grade point average was going to be borderline in keeping her scholarship. Her Psychology class was her worst grade. She asked her mentor for a suggestion. He knew the professor and that he was a kind and caring person. "Go see him and get his study suggestions and most of all, make sure he knows you care and are not just blowing off his class." She did and at the end of the semester she got the grade she needed in the class and knew that he had bumped her grade average up by a few points. She said, "That suggestion saved a $10,000 scholarship for me." Here is the deal: for some professors, it makes a difference, if they know you care. This is not true in every situation. One professor once said if he knew a student cared and they had been there most of the time, he would bump up a grade average a few points, if it would give them a better grade.

How do they know you care?

First, immediately go to the professor after the first test, if you have not done well and ask for study suggestions, etc. Going at the end of the semester just expresses desperation.

Second, Go to class all the time. The professor who said he would bump students up a few points also said, "If a student has not been to class regularly, I know they don't care, so why should I?

Going to class is one of the ways you show you care. Is this true with every college professor? No it is not. But, going to the prof for suggestions when you are not doing well and being there all the time still increases your likelihood of doing well in the class. And, who knows which one might give you the two or three point bump you need for the better grade?

TIP #54

EAT THE BIGGEST FROG FIRST

Will Rogers, the famous humorist said, "If you have to eat two frogs, eat the biggest one first." This is one of the secrets of getting more done or getting the most important things done. Using your time well or getting done what you need to can sometimes seem overwhelming. There are two little secrets that help. First, make a list of what needs to be done that day or week. Then, number them in order of importance. The most important is number one. The second most important is number two and on down the list. It is not about what is easiest, most enjoyable, or what others want you to do. If you ONLY get one thing done that day, it will be the most important. It will be the one that mattered most. That is what Rogers meant by eating the biggest frog first.

TIP #55

TAKING A TEST

1. **Always** read the directions carefully. Do not assume anything.
2. **Skip** over the questions you do not know.
3. **Answer** those you know and be aware of the time left in the period.
4. **Then**, consider the ones you think you might know and answer them.
5. **Go** to those that you do not know or are least confident about. Unless there is a penalty for wrong answers, never leave one blank. Put down an answer. If it is long written answer, write an answer that correlates to something from the material that could possibly relate to the question. Partial credit is always a possibility.
6. **Remember** that your first impression is usually the best. Do not change an answer unless you are certain your first answer was wrong.
7. **Review** all answers to make sure you answered as intended or marked the correct one.

As a Christian, it is always appropriate to pray that God would help you remember what you have studied and to be at your best.

TIP #56

WHEN MAKING A CLASS PRESENTATION

You may be an old hand at speaking in public to a group or doing a speech. If you are not, here are two tips to help in doing it and doing it as well as possible.

1. **Stand up in your room** or somewhere private and do the speech or presentation out loud exactly as you will do it in the class.
   Sometimes what we have in our head does not make sense when we say it out loud. Practicing out loud forces us to put it into words. It also helps to see how to transition from one thought or key idea to the next. If you will be using notes, have those exactly like they will be for the presentation. After going through it the first time, make any corrections to your notes or changes in wording or transitions from main point to main point.

2. **After corrections** to wording and notes, stand up and do it out loud at least one more time. That is the way it will be done in the presentation.

TIP #57

WHAT IF YOUR PROFESSOR IS NOT A CHRISTIAN?

At some point, you will possibly have a professor who is not a Christian and goes out of his or her way to be negative about Christians and faith. So, how do you handle it? First, realize that the professor may be an expert in his or her field, but that does not necessarily mean that the comments they make about faith or the Bible are accurate. Remember, just because you do not know the answer to a question does not mean there is not an answer. Second, do not be rude to the professor even though they may be negative toward you and what you believe. That will not help you in the class and will not help them change their mind about the Christian faith. If there is discussion around faith in the class, state your beliefs in a positive way. Do not be negative or critical toward those who think differently. If you listen to them, they are more likely to listen to you. One way to have a positive witness to the professor is to take the class seriously and be responsible. Blowing off the class and the professor because he or she is negative toward the Christian faith will not benefit you, your grade, or your possible influence on others in the class.

"Always be prepared to give an answer to everyone who asks you to give the reason for the hope you have. But do this with gentleness and respect." I Peter 3:15

31

TIP #58

THE PROFESSOR IS A JERK!

"The professor is a jerk." has been said by lots of freshmen. Sometimes it is true. But, at the end of the semester, he or she will give you a grade that will be on your transcript. There will not be an asterisk by it that says at the bottom of the page, "The Professor was a jerk." Either switch classes while you still can or learn to live with the professor and to the best of your ability do what she or he is asking. Arguing or blowing off assignments that are unreasonable will not harm the prof. It will hurt you. Adjust or get into a different class. Whatever you do, don't just start skipping the class. The more you miss, the more likely you are to fail the class.

TIP #59

FIND YOUR CLASSES EARLY

Before the first day of classes, look at your schedule and go find where each of the classes meet, both building and room. It will save time on that first day of class. Arriving late for the first class is never a good start with a professor. Too many freshmen have told the story of hurrying to a class and getting into the room and when the teacher starts, they realize they are in the wrong class. The choices then are to get up and make the walk of shame to the door or sit there the whole time pretending you belong there. Plus, if you stay, you are missing the correct class. Freshmen Orientation Manuals often have maps or there may be an electronic one that can be downloaded. Other freshmen will be impressed that first day as you walk across campus confidently knowing exactly where you are going. And, you don't have to make the walk of shame in front of a room full of freshmen laughing and glad that it is not them.

TIP #60

STUDY TIPS

1. **Set up a schedule** with regular study times and a regular place to study. Then, when you go to that place at that time, your mind is more likely to focus and be ready to study. Some believe it works better for your regular study place to be away from your room. Some suggest having a set place or cubicle in the library.
2. **Take advantage** of practice problems. Many courses have practice problems. They illustrate the main points.
3. **Find** a study group. Many courses have groups that meet on a regular basis to study and prepare. Checking with the department office can tell you if and when a study group or tutoring session meets.

4. **Find out** your professor's office hours and do not be afraid to go to her or him with your questions. Many colleges require teachers to post their hours on their door.
5. **Many professors** will be quick to answer questions by email. Make sure to know each prof's email.

TIP #61

WHAT TO DO IN CLASS

Besides going to class every time, what can you do to make a better grade?

1. **Sit** on the front row. It helps you pay attention and the teacher is more likely to know your name and feel like you care.
2. **Take notes**. It helps you listen and provides material to use in studying for a test. What a professor talks about usually reveals what they see as most important. Jot down main points or a summary of a statement.
3. **Enter into** class discussions. It helps with your understanding of the material and demonstrates your interest. It is easier to listen to others when you are involved.
4. **If** you still do not understand something that was discussed, ask the teacher about it when the class is over.

TIP #62

TIME BETWEEN CLASSES

The most wasted time on a college campus is the time between two classes. If you have an 8:00 to 9:00 class and a 10:00 to 11:00 class, what do you do in between? It is easy to walk to the student center and see who is hanging out. Or, you can walk to the library and review for the coming class or get the reading done that was just assigned in the class you just left. That time can still be relaxing. Just grab a drink and go to a regular quiet spot between the two classes. If your 8:00 o'clock class and your 10:00 o'clock class meet three times a week, that time between is three hours. If someone told you they could give you three extra hours a week, you would say hooray. You have it, if you will use that hour wisely. Using it may free you up for more fun activities in the evening.

TIP #63

BEST STUDENT OR WORST STUDENT?

For some, college classes are the first time they have never been "the smartest student in the class". For others, it can be a new beginning. Many who graduate from college and some with high honors, were not good students in high school. It is okay to not be the smartest student in the class and what you did in high school does not have to determine what you will do in college. That is up to you. One way to help and encourage you in making better grades, if you have not been a good student, is to make friends with students who want to make good grades. Do you know what they call a Med Student who made C's in Med School? Doctor!

TIP #64

GET OVER BEING CAPTAIN OF _____.

When you hit campus, it is time to get over your having been Captain of the Cheerleaders, Football team, Dance squad, or the Baseball team. That was a good experience. But, now is the time to look for what is next, not hang on to something that is in the past. You can be upset that no one knows how important you were in high school or start looking for new opportunities that can be even better than high school. So, put away the letter jacket or majorette pullover. Check out the different clubs and activities on campus. If sports were big for you in high school, find out how to sign up to play intramural sports.

HINT: Girls seem to do this better than guys. Come on guys, get on with life!

TIP #65

DOES IT MATTER IF YOU TAKE A FOUR YEAR VACATION FROM CHURCH?

You can always say, "I will go in the summers when I am at home." Or, "I will get real involved after college when I settle down somewhere." Here is the problem with that. College is the key time of becoming the adult you will be for the rest of your life. If your faith is significant to you, then that needs to be part of what shapes your adulthood. It is in college that many meet and decide on the person they will marry. Faith needs to be part of that experience and decision. Some of the toughest and life changing decisions will be made during college days. Do you want to make those decisions and choices apart from the encouragement, help, and teaching of a church where people will love and help you? If God is to be part of your future, then a good church needs to be part of your present.

TIP #66

WHY COLLEGE FRESHMEN DROP CHURCH

National studies show that 7 out of 10 high school seniors who were active in church do not connect to a church in college. Why is that? Do all these freshmen go to school planning to drop out? While some may go with the idea of dropping church, that is not what happens to most. Many do not connect to a church because they were not intentional about making it happen. They just assume it will fall into place. Decide and make a commitment that you will connect to a church for your own benefit. Do not look for or expect to find a church just like the one at home that you just left. No two churches are just alike. Different can be better or just different. Plan to go to church the first two Sundays that you are on campus. That helps get it into the pattern you are developing at school. Plus, most college churches have special welcome events those first Sundays. One of the great things about being part of a college church is that it can connect you to adult mentors and is often a chance to meet some of your professors in an informal way. A bonus is some of the older adults you meet at church just might invite you to their house for a home cooked meal.

TIP #67

HOW DO YOU PICK A CHURCH AT COLLEGE?

One of the easy temptations for a Christian student at college is to float around to different churches, go here on Sundays, go to that one for a special event, or go where a friend is going this Sunday. To get the most out of church at college and to grow as a Christian, it is best to pick a church and commit to it. Most college student friendly churches will introduce themselves during the first couple of weeks with special events on Sundays and other days and evening as well. Find out what different churches are doing at the start of the semester and plan your visits accordingly. Ask upperclassmen where they go and why. One thing to consider is what service opportunities does a church offer that might fit your interests or even tie into your planned major. Also, it is not unusual for college churches to hire part time student workers. Visit more than one church, if that is an option. It will help you sense more what connects with you and your needs. Then, make a choice and commit. Beware of the easy temptation to just go where most of your new friends are going. Go where you need to go.

TIP #68

WHICH CAMPUS MINISTRY FITS ME?

You may be fortunate enough to attend a college that has a variety of campus based Christian ministries and church college ministries. Some will be denominationally based such as Baptist,

Methodist, Pentecostal, Catholic, etc. Others will be more non-denominational. Almost all ministries are open to students of any and no religious background. Obviously, where you make friends or feel welcome is a huge factor in deciding whether to be involved. Other than that, does it matter where you connect? Every Christian group has some basic beliefs and doctrines from which they operate and are central to their teaching. Some will say, "We just teach the Bible." While that is usually true, it will be THEIR interpretation of the scripture and what it means. Different Christian groups make different applications from the same scriptures. It is wise after visiting and becoming interested to consider, "How do their basic beliefs coincide with what I believe?" If you are not clear about it, ask your pastor or youth minister back home for help in making your decision. The main thing is to pick one and connect!

TIP #69

GET A CHURCH BUDDY.

One of the things that can keep a freshman from going to and getting involved in a church is having to go alone. That is sometimes hard and uncomfortable. When you make a commitment that you plan to attend and connect to a church, find a "Church Buddy". One place to find such a friend is at the Welcome Week events sponsored by the Christian ministries on campus. That is another reason to look for and be aware of these events on campus. After visiting churches, you and your Church Buddy may decide that different churches work best for each of you. That is okay. After visiting a church and attending some of their events, you will likely have met some other students that go there. So, you can be comfortable going alone knowing you will see these new friends when you get there. Or, you can develop a new Church Buddy that attends there. One way to have a Church Buddy is to invite someone to go with you anytime you plan to go.

"Therefore encourage one another and build each other up..." I Thessalonians 5:11a

TIP #70

EVERY DAY

College is a great time to start the habit of reading the Bible every day, if you have not already. The Bible is full of encouragement and wisdom for every day life that God has inspired for us. The best way to read every day is to have a set time to do it. Many do it the first thing each day, but that is up to you. It does not have to be long. Simply plan to take a few minutes to read scripture and then to pray briefly. First, what do you read? There are all of kinds of great devotional books or Bible reading plans. Many churches have reading or devotional plans they will give you. Some of these plans guide you in reading through the whole Bible in a year. But, you can also just start on your own. One way would be to start with a short book like Philippians which has just four brief chapters and read a chapter or part of a chapter each day. Or, you could start with the book of Acts, which is the story of the beginnings of the Christian church. The Old Testament book of Proverbs has 31 chapters and some read a chapter of it on the day of the month corresponding with the chapter number. What should you pray? You can ask God to help you be aware of his presence in your life that day and pray for family and friends who have individual needs. What if you miss a day or two? Just pick up where you left off and go on from there. You may be surprised how these brief few minutes can give you more awareness of God's work and will in your life.

All scripture is God-breathed and is useful for teaching, rebuking, correcting and training in righteousness." II Timothy 3:16

TIP #71

WHEN YOU ARE DISCOURAGED OR DEPRESSED

Everyone gets discouraged at some time or other. That just means you are normal. The main thing is to not let that control you or to continue to feel that way.

So, what do you do? Two tips:

1. **Talk to someone** you trust such as an older friend, mentor, a school counselor, or a College Minister. Just talking about it with someone can help put things in perspective. Discouragement is often a result of not seeing things in proper perspective. It may be the result of a temporary setback or the strain from adjusting to all the new school throws at you. Talking it out with someone helps us know we are not alone. Every college campus has a Counseling Center or a designated Counselor and it is free. Going there does not mean you are crazy or weird. It means you like all of us do have simply hit a rough spot.

2. **It is easier** to act your way into a better way of feeling than it is to feel your way into a better way of acting. What that means is, when we are discouraged or blue, it is easy to withdraw and not go on with normal activities. Even though you may not feel like getting out and doing things often, if you will, your feelings will catch up with your positive actions. Do not wait until "the feeling" strikes you

TIP #72

SHARE SOME PRIVATE THINGS.....HOWEVER

Sometimes we need to share something very private in order to clear our head, heart, and soul. But, here is the thing, be wise in whom you confide. Some friends are great to go with to a movie or ballgame and have a great time. But, they tend to tell everybody everything they know. If it is really private and important, you might share it with one college age friend that you KNOW can keep confidences and will love you no matter what. A step above that is to talk it out with an older mentor, your pastor, etc. Once you have shared something, it cannot be taken back. Be wise in what you share and with whom you share it. Many students have quickly lived to regret those late night "share sessions" in the dorm. Don't be one of them.

TIP #73

GO HOME......JUST NOT EVERY WEEKEND

If you are living at school and away from home, your parents miss you and want to see you. You want to see home friends and sleep in your own bed. Part of doing well at school is developing some good and positive relationships. Weekend activities at school are good relationship builders. Fun things (and some bad things) happen on the weekend. If you go to a school that has football, plan to be there for the first home game, even if you are not a football fan. On most campuses students get in free or at a reduced rate. Go with a group and have a good time. Lots of organizations like campus ministry groups have tailgate parties before the game. Or, get three or four new friends together and have your own tailgate with stuff you make yourself or pick up on the way. Your group can get under a tree somewhere near the stadium, eat, and get to know each other better. Lots of college ministry churches do special things on football weekends too. You do not have to know what a first down is to have a good time and make more and deeper friendships on a football weekend in the fall. But, things like that cannot happen, if you go home every weekend.

TIP #74

SUMMERS ARE PRECIOUS

Not only does summer bring an end to what sometimes seems like a long Spring Semester, it also provides opportunities. It is a good idea to some time in your freshman year to develop a plan as to what you will do with your precious three or four summers. Summers can provide new and growing experiences that help you develop in your field and or as a person. If you are a Christian, one option to seriously consider is to spend at least one summer serving in a mission opportunity. Many of these are partially or fully funded both in the U.S. and abroad. Your church or campus ministry can tell you what these opportunities are. Some majors require a summer of internship prior to senior year. Internships not only give good experience in your chosen field, but also open up the possibilities for future employment with those companies after graduation. If you are in school a long way from home, parents usually would love it, if you would spend at least one summer at home before graduation. Start out with a plan for your summers. You can always adjust it as you go along, but you cannot ever get a summer back.

TIP #75

PARENTS' NUMBER ONE COMPLAINT

Parents number one complaint about and with their freshman is lack of communication and especially related to tests, grades, and major decisions. While some freshmen "over-communicate" in asking parents what to do and what decision to make in every situation, many are just the opposite. It is only reasonable that parents would be interested and concerned about how you are doing your first semester at college. One way to resolve this issue to set a time to have a "visit call" each week. For example, some freshmen call home every Sunday afternoon. They let parents know what is going on school wise, social life, or whatever. You know your family schedule best. When is a good time to tell your parents you will call every week? It could be Sunday afternoon, Tuesday night, or early one morning. Do whatever works for your family schedule. Parents want to hear from you other than when you need extra money. That complaint can be easily handled.

TIP #76

UNDERSTANDING AND WORKING WITH PARENTS

Going away to college may seem to bring additional conflict between you and your parents. Why is that? First, understand this is a life change for them also. It signals them moving out of one stage of their life to another. Second, it is a time of concern for them. They know how much this new experience will shape and affect your life. In many ways, they see that more clearly than you do. So, their fear antenna is way up.

Here are ways to work with your parents for a more positive relationship:

1. **Keep in mind** that you going to college is a major adjustment for them also. In many cases parents are sacrificing financially to make this possible and that increases the concern for them.

2. **Communication** is the most important thing you can do. Let them know in advance decisions you are considering and why.
3. **Do not** spring major decisions on your parents without advance warning and discussion.
4. **Demonstrate** you are being wise about your budgeting and expenditures.
5. **Keep** them in the loop. Let them know what is going on, especially in the first few weeks.
6. **IF** you are attending school away from home, invite them to come to an event such as Homecoming or Parents Weekend. It allows them to see how you are doing and shows you have appreciation for them.

"Honor your father and mother, so that you may live long in the land the Lord your God is giving you." Exodus 20:12

TIP #77

HOW CAN I KNOW GOD'S WILL FOR MY LIFE?

Some ask about God's will and others simply ask how to know what vocation to pursue as their life's work. God cares about everything that we do and that we are:

Some signs in knowing what to do with your life:

1. **What** do people tell you that you do well? God's will for our life is usually written into who we are.
2. What do you get the most joy or **satisfaction** from doing? Some things we do just naturally connect to who we are.
3. What do you see that **needs doing** and moves you? Sometimes, God speaks to us in the needs that we see around us.
4. **Try** some different things. Different experiences either give us affirmation or help us realize that is not something we are wired to do as a major part of our life.
5. **Ask** a wise older friend such as a pastor or College Minister. They cannot and will not tell you what you ought to do with your life, but they can help you process and work through your thoughts and experiences. They may be able to point out the obvious.

"For we are God's workmanship created in Christ Jesus to do good works, which God prepared in advance for us to do. Ephesians 2:10

TIP #78

BEING A CONTAGIOUS CHRISTIAN

College is a great place for God to use you in the life of others. Plus, you will grow in your faith while doing it. Someone who is contagious has an effect on others. God uses our relationships to affect others.

Here are some ways to be contagious:

1. **Be intentional.** Make the conscious decision that you want God to use you during your freshman year. Pray that He will show you opportunities.
2. **Stay connected.** As you try to be all God wants you to be, it is more important than ever to stay connected to church, a college ministry and Christian friends that will encourage you.
3. **Beware** of the danger of involvement with non-Christians to the extent that they have more influence on you than you do on them.
4. **Be real.** When we are trying to impact others for Christ, an easy temptation is to try to project a super Christianity or pretend to be more than we are. Be genuine.
5. **Connect** to a mentor. Find a mature Christian who will meet with you regularly to encourage and help you learn more about the Lord and helping others.

QUICK TIPS FROM FORMER FRESHMEN WHO SURVIVED

TIP #79

Learn about nutrition. Your mind will work better when you are eating real food." Margaret

TIP #80

You need to belong...be in band, or choir, or other organizations." Robby

TIP #81

When you make a decision, ask someone who has done it before. Never make a decision without asking six who are experts in the area." Conway

TIP #82

"Some of the friends you make your freshman year will be for life. Choose Carefully." Jim

TIP #83

70% of high school seniors drop out of church, even though it was not intentional. Develop a strong relationship with another believer early on to keep each other accountable." Mike

TIP #84

"Study hard.....but don't let your studies interfere with your education.....believe it or not, this was from my father." Bill

TIP #85

"Make sure the professors know who you are and don't take 8:00 a.m. classes." Josh

TIP #86

"You are normal." Brian

TIP #87

"Get involved in two extra curricular groups.....one a Christian campus ministry and one other group (sports, drama, music, etc.)." Mel

TIP #88

"Be sure you set aside some time for activities that help you relax and take the stress out of your day or week." Les

TIP #89

"Drink more water. (Eighty ounces of Mountain Dew per day is really unhelpful.) Chase

TIP #90

"Always take an easy A for an elective and don't miss two classes in the same day." Nathanie

TIP #91

Get enough sleep." Kiki

TIP #92

"My Aunt and Uncle told me one of the most important things was to find a college church. I did and they were right." Mark

TIP #93

"Don't go home for the first month of fall semester." Kim

TIP #94

"Take care of your body, you will be stuck with it for a while. Eat smart, sleep, laugh, and pray." Jim

TIP #95

"Take classes with Department Heads when possible...not graduate instructors. Don't be afraid to seek help from professors unless you have not been going to class." Bill

TIP #96

"Call your mom and dad. They miss you." Ward

TIP #97

"Don't go back home every weekend! Invest in your new friends and relationships because they may end up being your most important ones later in life." Haila

TIP #98

"It's okay to get mad at God....and to say to Him, 'God, I'm mad at you.' Just don't stay mad at God." Phil

TIP #99

"Find a good Bible teaching church that will get you through all the other mess! Be an encourager to others." Lisa

TIP #100

"Don't go through Rush till sophomore year. Get to know the programs from a distance without the pressure." Missy

TIP #101

"If upperclassmen ask you to do the 'Milk Challenge" don't!" C. J.

(The "Milk Challenge" is to guzzle a gallon of milk and see who can hold it down the longest before throwing up.)

TIP #102

"Get involved in clubs! Meet people! Put yourself out there and engage with quality people." Cissy

TIP #103

"A college degree doesn't guarantee immediate job placement. Get an internship. Also, make sure there is a demand for your chosen profession." Jennifer

TIP #104

"Learn time management." Bob

TIP #105

"The world is not like your household and you'll lose some of the protection, but there are good people out there, find them by being connected with your church and university ministry." Daniel

TIP #106

"Get some experience in the field you want to work in before graduation. Job shadow, do an internship, Volunteer. Make sure it is what you really want to do." Laura

TIP #107

"Start planning into your college career doing short term missions, summer service, or a gap year. It will be some of the best education you receive." Jerry

TIP #108

"If you don't have a clear direction, don't declare a major. Take basics the first few semesters, then declare. Switching major costs time and money. I know...did it twice!" Bryan

TIP #109

"Don't open a credit card to get a free tee shirt." Kyle

TIP #110

"You don't know until you ask. Don't meet the prerequisite but know you can do the class, ask. Have two classes you need that overlap, ask. Struggling with a class, aaaassk! Professors are allies and want you to succeed." Alexandra

TIP #111

"Listen to your parents and seek godly wisdom, not knowledge alone." Ron

TIP #112

"When you aren't sure what to do, keep doing what you already know to do. Go to church and read your Bible." Lori

TIP #113

"If you make a decision and it begins to look like it's not a good choice, don't be afraid to make a different choice (again and again is ok)." Joann

TIP #114

"Your witness on campus starts in the classroom….you can't preach Jesus to a professor in whose class you are failing to show effort. You can't expect profs and classmates to respect your beliefs when you disrespect them with the approach you take to the classes in which they are invested." Jon

TIP #115

"Always go to bed in the same day you wake up. A Baylor Dean said, 'Let your day be 9 to 5. Study between classes." Alana

TIP #116

"Do a little more than is expected." Melissa

TIPS FROM SCRIPTURE AND GREAT FOR MEMORIZING

TIP #117

"Do your best to present yourself to God as one approved, a workman who does not need to be ashamed and who correctly handles the word of truth. 2 Timothy 2:15

TIP #118

"Flee the evil desires of youth and pursue righteousness, faith, love, and peace......don't have anything to do with foolish and stupid arguments because you know they produce quarrels." 2 Timothy 2:22-23

TIP #119

"Whatever you do, work at it with all your heart, as working for the Lord, not for men." Colossians 3:23

TIP #120

"Being confident of this, that he who began a good work in you will carry it on to completion until the day of Christ Jesus." Philippians 1:6

TIP #121

"Whatever happens, conduct yourselves in a manner worthy of the gospel of Christ." Philippians 1:27

TIP # 122

"I can do everything through him who gives me strength." Colossians 4:13

TIP #123

"Do not conform any longer to the pattern of this world, but be transformed by the renewing of your mind. Then you will be able to test and approve what God's will is, his good, pleasing and perfect will." Romans 12:2

TIP #124

"Do not think of yourself more highly than you ought, but rather think of yourself with sober judgement, in accordance with the measure of faith God has given you. Romans 12:3b

Arliss is married to Sue whom he began to date after running for president of the student body in college and losing by four votes. Soon after they began to date, he learned that Sue had voted against him. They have two daughters and two granddaughters. You can email Arliss at arlissdickerson@gmail.com.

Arliss has published a variety of college ministry books that are available at amazon.com/books.

49